Delphi

Publishers: George A. Christopoulos, John C. Bastias
Translation: Brian de Jongh
Special Photography: Spyros Tsavdaroglou and Makis Skiadaresis, Nikos Kontos
Colour separation: Pietro Carlotti.

Delphi

MANOLIS ANDRONICOS

Professor of Archaeology at the University of Thessalonike

EKDOTIKE ATHENON S.A.
Athens 2002

ISBN 960-213-033-4
Copyright © 1976
by
EKDOTIKE ATHENON S.A.
1, Vissarionos Street
Athens 106 72, Greece

PRINTED AND BOUND IN GREECE
by
EKDOTIKE HELLADOS S.A.
An affiliated company
8, Philadelphias Street, Athens

DELPHI AND THE MUSEUM

DELPHI

The first diviner to occupy the Delphic oracle was the mother of the gods, Gaia. She was succeeded by her daughter, Themis. The third occupant was another daughter of Gaia, the Titaness Phoibe, who gave Apollo the surname of Phoibos as a birthday present. We have this information from the Pythia's own mouth, in the opening lines of Aischylos' tragedy *Eumenides*. As regards the rest of the story: how Apollo founded his first temple at Delphi, and how he slew the fearful dragon (a female serpent) near a spring, this is recounted in the ancient Homeric hymn to Apollo. In later times, men believed this serpent to have been male and even more redoubtable, none other than the famous Python, guardian of Gaia's oracle; the battle that the young god who had come from the north — from the valley of Tempe — fought against the serpent was indeed a great and terrible one. They also believed that although a god, Apollo complied to the divine rule which he himself had set: that whoever defiled his hands with the blood of murder should be sent into exile. Thus the god departed for eight years and worked in the service of Admetos, King of Pherai, in order to cleanse himself of the pestilent blood of murder; then he returned, purified and clean at last, sole master of the Delphic oracle.

This is what the ancients had to say about the beginnings of the legendary oracle. But concerning the site itself, that unique site which overwhelms whoever visits it for the first time, they had another story to tell. Zeus, wishing to find the centre of the earth, let loose two eagles from the two ends of the world; the sacred birds met at Delphi, which meant that there was the "navel" of the earth. Hence, Apollo's sanctuary contained, since remotest times, an *omphalos* (navel-stone), and votive offerings in the shape of the *omphalos* were presented to the god by pious pilgrims from all over the world (fig. 17). The Apollonian oracle was indeed celebrated and venerated throughout the inhabited world. Not only Greeks, but barbarian monarchs as well sent envoys to consult the oracle and expressed their gratitude by dedicating sumptuous gifts and votive offerings to the god.

The Site

Such are the myths of the ancients concerning Apollo, Delphi and the celebrated oracle. However, before we come to the Delphic sanctuary and speak of the Delphic cult, we must first take a look at the place itself — the place which was once behind to be the centre of the earth (fig. 2). The usual approach to Delphi by land is by means of the road climbing up from Boiotia towards Arachova and then descending westward; it is the same road which the god himself followed when he first came to Delphi, as we are informed by the Homeric hymn to Apollo. Another approach is by means of the Corinthian gulf, and that was the one used by the first priests of Apollo, who were Cretans. Now the visitor encounters a landscape vividly described in the Homeric hymn: "You climbed rapidly (Phoibos is being addressed here) running across the hill-tops and you reached the regions of Krisa below Mount Parnassos which is covered with much snow, at the point where it forms a knee to the west, and a large rock overhangs the spot, while below a wild valley stretches out; this was the spot where the Lord Phoibos Apollo decided to have a beautiful temple . . ."

Anybody coming upon the holy site for the first time is struck with awe. "It is as if the earth had been cleft asunder by some cosmogonic spasm; the valley is a vast and profound chasm... And as soon as we reach the foot of the Phaidriades, at the exact spot of the Kastalian Spring, we are faced with something that appears like the chasm of chasms: the two rocks are separated by a tremendous gorge, narrow and impassable — the Arkoudorema (the Bear's Gully) as it is known today — which continues all the way down the slope, deep into the thicket" (Ch. Karouzos). And there, at the point where the two rocks meet, in the deepest recess of the gorge and at the foot of the east rock (known anciently as Hyampeia and presently as Flempoukos), the most limpid water gushes forth: it is the water of the celebrated Kastalian Fountain where both priests and pilgrims cleansed themselves before entering the temple (fig. 11). On the western side, at the foot of the rock named Rhodini, Apollo's sanctuary, the most famous in ancient Greece, extends across the opening on the rising ground (fig. 6). And down below, the deep valley of the Pleistos river spreads out, green and silver with olive-groves, and merges with the plain of Itea stretching all the way down to the sea-coast (fig. 2).

The history of Delphi

The history of Delphi is inextricably bound with the history of the sanctuary and the oracle; to be more precise, Delphi only existed as a township under the shadow of the sanctuary. Archaeological excavations have revealed the existence of an insignificant settlement on the site of the sanctuary and further east, dating back to c. 1400 B.C. This settlement was destroyed at the end of the Mycenaean period, but came back to life in Geometric times, when Apollo's cult began to take root in that region. Hence-forward, Delphi acquired world fame and power of a kind unparalleled in Greece, although it remained a small town, sparsely populated. Over the course of 250 years, four sacred wars were waged for this small town, and at the end it caused the annihilation of the Phokians.

The Amphiktyonies

It is no easy task to embrace the whole history of Delphi in a few lines, or to interpret the significance of the Delphic oracle since the earliest times of antiquity. Nevertheless, one should point out the fact that the Delphic oracle was by no means neutral to the historic destiny of Hellenism, nor did it restrict itself to the passive role of handing out prophetic advice. In a way that was unique and very nearly inexplicable to people of our times, the Delphic contribution to wartime and peacetime enterprises, to political and civil controversies, to intellectual and religious pursuits, was always highly relevant and decisive in the context of the Greek world. There is one fundamental factor, however, which may shed some light on the unique position occupied by the Pythian sanctuary in Greek history. In central Greece there existed an Amphiktyony whose seat was the sanctuary of Demeter at Anthele, a small town near Thermopylai. In the 7th century B.C., the seat of the Amphiktyony was transferred to the sanctuary of Apollo at Delphi. The Amphiktyonic League, then, declared Delphi an independent township — which meant that it no longer came under the Phokian state — and placed the sanctuary under its own protection. There existed similar Amphiktyonies in other parts of Greece as well. However, the Amphiktyony of Delphi did not consist of delegations from the city-states, but from the "nations" of the Hellenes, in other words, the ancient tribes that made up the main body of ancient Hellenism: Ainianes, Achaians, Phthiotians, Dolopes, Dorians, Thessalians, Ionians, Lokrians, Malians, Magnetes, Perrhaibians, Phokians. And so the sanctuary of Apollo became the religious and political centre of the Hellenic world — a position which no other sanctuary could claim.

The growing fame of the Delphic Oracle

During the peak period of Greek colonization (late 8th-7th century B.C.), Greek cities that had resolved to establish a colony to some distant land first consulted the oracle as to where they should go and who should become the *oikistes,* the leader and founder of the future colony. Syracuse, Kroton, Kyrene, Thasos are among the better-known of many colonies that owed their very existence to the wise counsel of Phoibos. Several other colonies chose to name themselves after the god: Apollonia. All these cities honoured Apollo with the surname of *Archegetes,* meaning first leader. Thus the prestige and fame of the god and his oracle spread East and West, far beyond the bounds of metropolitan Greece. As early as the 7th century B.C., Midas, the legendary king of Phrygia, sent his own royal throne to the Pythian Apollo as a token of his veneration. At about the same time, another legendary king, Gyges (675 B.C.), founder of the Mermnad dynasty and ancestor of Croesus, dedicated magnificent votive offerings of pure gold to the Delphic god. Kypselos, the renowned wealthy tyrant of Corinth, built in the Delphic sanctuary the first "treasury", i.e. a small building in the shape of a temple, which had the double function of serving as a votive offering and sheltering the smaller, precious offerings dedicated by each city to the sanctuary.

The glory, power and wealth of the Delphic oracle grew steadily. However, it appears that the Phokians of Krisa decided to exploit their position as neighbours to Delphi, and levied heavy dues on the faithful who disembarked at the port of Kirrha, in Phokian territory, on their way to the oracle. Delphi then appealed to the Amphiktyony for help and the First Sacred War was declared. It was to last ten years, ending in 591 B.C. with the annihilation of the Krisaians. Kirrha and Krisa were destroyed and their territory was dedicated to the Delphic deities. The Amphiktyons then proceeded to reorganize the Pythian festival, which took place every 8 years to commemorate Apollo's return from his voluntary exile after the slaying of Python. From 582 B.C. this festival was celebrated every four years; gymnastic and equestrian contests were added to the earlier musical competition.

The sanctuary's fame spread across the world, and the offerings it received were beyond anything the boldest imagination might conceive. Croesus, the king of Lydia, famous for his wealth, sent all kinds of offerings, the most sumptuous being a lion of solid gold weighing about 250 kgs., set upon a pyramid made of 117 bricks of "white gold" (a mixture of gold and silver); in addition to that, two large kraters, one gold and the other silver, which were placed to the right and left of the temple entrance. When Apollo's poros temple was destroyed by fire in 548 B.C., not only the Greeks, but foreign sovereigns, such as Croesus of Lydia and Amasis of Egypt, made generous donations for the construction of a new temple, which cost 300 talents, the equivalent of several billions of present-day drachmae. The Alkmeonidai, the noble Athenian family exiled by Peisistratos and his sons, undertook the construction project; in excess of what was stipulated in the contract, they used marble for the façade instead of poros.

During the critical years of the Persian Wars, the oracle was considerably shaken by the power of the invaders; its prophecies and advice did not reflect that high moral character so representative of the Greeks who fought "in defence of all". The sanctuary itself escaped Persian plundering through the god's miraculous intervention: enormous rocks rolled down the cliffs of the Phaidriades and caused the enemy to disperse in panic. The oracle may have shown a slight weakening in the moment of crisis, but the faith of the Greeks in Phoibos remained steadfast; with the ever-burning flame of the temple they rekindled the desecrated altars of the sanctuaries and sent him magnificent votive offerings, among which the famous gold tripod, set upon a bronze pedestal 6 metres high, consisting of three intertwined snakes, engraved with the names of the 31 cities that fought against the Persians in Plataia.

About the middle of the 5th century B.C., the Phokians once again gained political power over Delphi; this led to the declaration of the Second Sacred War (447 B.C.), to restorethe sanctuary's independence. In 373 B.C., a terrible earthqyake uprooted huge pieces of rock and flung them on the temple of Apollo. Reconstruction started immediately, thanks to pan-Hellenic contributions, but it was interrupted in 356 B.C. by a Third Sacred War. The Phokians occupied the sanctuary for a period of ten years and confiscated not only sanctuary funds, but also a large number of valuable votive offerings. The Greeks felt highly idignant at this sacrilege. Following the intervention of Philip, king of Macedonia, the Phokians were routed, excluded from the Amphyktyony and obliged to pay a colossal indemnity (420 talents). Finally, the Fourth Sacred War broke out in 339 B.C., against the Lokrians this time. Once again, Philip assumed leadership; after defeating the Lokrians, he proceeded to Chaironeia, where he fought the famous battle (338 B.C.), which made him master of Greece.

The Hellenistic period

During the Hellenistic period, the Greek world underwent a radical transformation. The old faith was shaken; the cities gradually lost their independence and merged within the larger context of great kingdoms. The powerful kings began to rely on their own armies rather than on divine assistance. They still consulted the oracle and sent rich gifts, but this was done in a wish to display their own wealth rather than honour the god. In 279 B.C. once again with the miraculous assistance of Apollo, Delphi was saved from the brutal invasion of the Galatians. To commemorate this event, the Aitolians — who now ruled the area — instituted a new annual festival, the *Soteria* (Salvation festival). This invasion is mentioned in one of the two Delphic hymns engraved on the walls of the Treasury of the Athenians; these hymns have become famous because the musical notation that accompanied them has survived in the intervals between the lines. The kings of Pergamon, well-known for their generosity and love of the arts, built stoas, restored the old wall-paintings by Polygnotos, sent numerous offerings, but also made sure that their statues occupied a prominent position in the sanctuary.

The desecration and decline of the sanctuary

In 168 B.C. the Roman Aemilius Paulus defeated the Macedonians at Pydna; and at Delphi, upon the pedestal which Perseus, the Macedonian king, had prepared for his statue, the Roman set up his own equestrian figure (fig. 7). The hour of Rome had come. In 86 B.C., Sulla removed all the valuable offerings that had survived the Fourth Sacred War; and in 83 B.C., barbarians from Thrace plundered the sanctuary and set fire to the temple; this was the first time, according to tradition, when the flame burning since time immemorial was extinguished, depriving both Greeks and barbarians of its beneficient radiance. Nevertheless, the Delphic sanctuary still prospered; Nero removed no less than 500 statues from Delphi; and yet when Pausanias visited it in the 2nd century A.D., he still found it full of masterpieces. However, when the Roman emperors were converted to Christianity, the ancient religion no longer had any place in the new State. Constantine the Great took away from Delphi innumerable works of art for the embellishment of his new capital; among these was the famous offering of the Greeks for their vixtory at Plataia; its base can still be seen today not far from Hagia Sophia. Theodosios the Great prohibited the ancient cult and games in A.D. 394. And when Julian, the most romantic of emperors, sent Oreibasios to consult the Pythia at Delphi, the prophetess uttered her last oracle, as a kind of epitaph for the ancient sanctuary:

> *"Tell ye the King: the carven hall is fallen in decay;*
> *Apollo hath no chapel left, no prophesying bay,*
> *No talking spring. The stream is dry and had so much to say."*

The method of divination

The fame and power of Delphi was based on its oracle, which was one of the oldest in Greece. Nearly all ancient authors mention it at some point, or record some story or incident relating to it. Nevertheless, it would be a mistake to believe that we possess all the information we would wish to have, of all the details we consider necessary, concerning the procedure of divination at Delphi. A great many problems remain unsolved and numerous questions have not yet found an answer. We shall try, therefore, to set down as briefly as possible the results of recent research into the methods of divination at the Delphic oracle.

According to ancient tradition, Panassos, the eponymous hero of Mount Parnassos, discovered the art of reading auguries in the flight of birds: Delphos, the hero of the city Delphi, was the first to teach entrail-reading. and Amphiktyon, the hero of the Amphiktyony, introduced oneiromancy (dream-interpretation). We also know that there existed in the Delphic sanctuary a body priests named *Pyrkooi,* who could read auguries in the flames of sacrificial pyres. The Delphic myths mention the existence of nymphs known as Thriai — in ancient Greek this word denotes the pebbles used in divination; one can therefore assume that these nymphs were simply the personification of divination by lot. The Delphic myths provide clear enough evidence that every known method of divination was practised at Delphi. But Delphi owed its fame to the oracles delivered by the Pythia, who received direct inspiration from Apollo and spoke in his name; in other words, the god of divination himself delivered the oracle, using the Pythia as a medium.

The Pythia was a woman over 50 years old. She was not necessarily a virgin, bur from the moment she undertook this highest of duties — serving the god — she was under the obligation to abandon her husband and children, to move into a house destined for her alone, within the sacred precinct, to be chaste and irreproachable, and to observe certain religious rules. In spite of her age, she wore the garments of a young girl, as a mark of the virginal purity of her life. We do not know how the Pythia was selected; but it is quite certain that she did not have to belong to a noble family, like the priests and priestesses who served at other Greek sanctuaries; nor did she have to go through special training or education. She was a simple, ordinary peasant-woman, without any distinguishing mark until the moment Apollo allowed his inspiration to descend upon her. In the beginning there was only one Pythia; but when the requirements of the oracle grew more numerous, two more Pythias were added.

Until the Classical period, nobody had ever thought of questioning the Pythia's sudden transformation and the fact that Phoibos spoke through her. All that has been written about the natural vapours emanating from the chasm in the sanctuary, or about the laurel leaves the Pythia munched and the water she drand is but an attempt to find answers to the mystery, at a time when the faithful began to lose their faith, thinking they could explain the divine miracle with the cold instrument of reason and encompass the supernatural within a recognizable human measure. However, the ancient Greeks were certain of one thing alone: the importance of Apollo's sacred tripod, in other words, his throne, which had once been equipped with wings and carried him across land and sea. Why had Apollo chosen such an unusual throne, nobody knew and nabody dared ask; nor have any modern scholars provided a certain answer to that question. It was upon this throne that the Pythia sat in order to become the god's instrument. It was enough for her to take Apollo's place, to shed her ordinary identity, fall into a trance and deliver the divine messages in a series of mysterious, inarticulate cries. But before the Pythia took her seat upon the tripod, it was necessary to find out whether the god consented to her practising divination. A goat was therefore brought to sacrifice; but before sacrificing it, the animal was sprinkled with cold water: if it shivered from head to foot, it meant the god consented; if it did not, then the Pythia could not sit on the oracular tripod.

In early antiquity, before the 6th century B.C., divination took place only once a year, on the seventh day of the month Bysios (February-March), on Apollo's birthday. Later on it took place every month, again on the seventh day of the month, except for the three winter months, because during that time the god left the Delphic sanctuary in order to travel far away to the land of the Hyperboreans, conceding his place to Dionysos, who was worshipped next to Apollo in his own temple. On the sacred day appointed for divination, the Pythia was the first to visit at dawn the Kastalian Spring to cleanse herself. Then she burnt laurel leaves on the sacred hearth and immersed herself in smoke. Meanwhile the priests prepared the sacrificial goat; if the god gave his consent, the animal was sacrificed on the great altar — a dedication of the Chians — in front of the temple, and thus all the pilgrims knew an oracle would be delivered that day at Delphi. In the meantime, the *Prophetai* and the *Hosioi* (priests of both Apollo and Dionysos) and certain delegates from the township of Delphi also cleansed themselves in the sacred waters of Kastalia. Finally, all the pilgrims who wished to consult the oracle similarly purified themselves at the spring.

When everyone was ready, they advanced in a festive procession towards the temple, filled with awe and anticipation. Delegates from the cities (*theopropoi*) and private individuals stood outside the temple and offered the *pelanos* at the altar — a kind of consecrated bread sold on the spot at a high price, the pilgrims' first contribution to the sanctuary. Then they each advanced in turn towards the temple and placed a slaughtered animal as an offering upon the inner altar, where the undying flame burned. It was considered a great privilege to be the first to receive an oracle; this was known as 'promanteia'. The priority was always retained by the people of Delphi for their own city, but second place was offered as the highest sign of honour to cities and individuals who had proved worthy of it.

The Pythia was already seated on the tripod in the *adyton* or inner shrine. The *Prophetai* stood nearby, and the pilgrim — it could only be a man — sat in a corner at some distance from her, having already posed his question to one of the *Prophetai,* either in writing or orally. The Pythia, hidden by some kind of partition, was not visible to anyone. The *Prophetes* put the question to her and she would give the god's response, deep in her trance. This was apparently unintelligible to others, but the *Prophetes* was able to comprehend it and write it down in hexameter verse; it was this written reply that was handed over to the pilgrim. The equivocal replies of the Delphic oracle have become famous in history; they were so obscure, so incomprehensible that additional divinatory gifts were required to interpret them correctly and avoid unfortunate mistakes. The case of Croesus is a good example: in answer to his question, the god said that if he waged war on the Persians, he would destroy a great power; he never suspected that *Loxias* (a surname of Apollo, meaning the Oblique One, because of the ambiguous replies he was giving) meant to convey that he would destroy his own kingdom if he fought the Persians.

Those nine days of the year when the Pythia spoke with the voice of the god must have had a tremendous impact on the pilgrims fortunate enough to be present in the Delphic sanctuary. Only a very small percentage of those who wished to consult the divine oracle had the privilege of receiving an answer within those nine days in the year when divination was performed. For this reason, since the Archaic age, most of the pilgrims' questions were answered in a different manner: by drawing lots. This kind of divination took place every day of the year, not in the *adyton,* but in public view; it was the most common method of divination as regards simple and concrete questions, that is to say questions that could be answered by a simple affirmative or negative. But when we refer to the Pythia and the celebrated oracles delivered at Delphi, we have in mind those great days, when the god himself let his voice be heard through the mouth of the entranced prophetess.

THE SANCTUARIES:
The Sanctuary of Athena Pronaia

Before reaching the Delphic sanctuary proper, we come upon the sanctuary of Athena Pronaia (now called Marmaria), situated on a narrow terrace on the left-hand side of the road looking down the valley of the Pleistos river. In remote antiquity, this must have been a place where some goddess was worshipped, as attested by the discovery of numerous Mycenaean figurines representing a goddess with outstretched arms. This sanctuary was later dedicated to Athena: it was she, together with Phylakos, a local hero, who guarded the sanctuary and temple of Apollo; hence she was given the name of *Pronaia,* i.e. the goddess who stood before the temple.

The remains of only a few buildings have survived within the enclosure of the sanctuary; but they are among the finest examples of ancient Greek architecture. They include the Archaic temple of Athena (built around 650 B.C.), which is one of the oldest monumental temples known to us. On the same site, but larger, was the second Archaic temple (built around 500 B.C.). Like the first one, it was a Doric *peripteros* constructed of poros, with a surrounding colonnade of 6 columns on the ends and 12 columns at the sides. It had a front porch (*pronaos*) and an extensive cella (*sekos*), but no rear porch (*opisthodomos*). The floor of the *pteron,* from the outer colonnade to the walls of the cella, was paved with coloured pebbles. As already mentioned, in the years of the Persian Wars, a devastating earthquake caused the fall of gigantic rocks from the Phaidriades, which damaged the sanctuary of Athena Pronaia; one of these rocks can be seen today among the altars, east of the temple. This was perhaps the reason why a wall was built to reinforce the columns of the NE corner of the temple. In the 4th century B.C., however, this temple too was destroyed and only its ruins have survived to the present. A natural disaster of a different kind from that which caused panic to the Persians 2,500 years ago, and to the Galatians at a later date, occurred at Delphi and the site of Athena's sanctuary in the early years of our century. In March 1905, huge rocks were swept away by torrential rains from the cliff of Hyampeia and fell upon the ruins of the temple, demolishing 12 of the surviving 15 columns. It is probable that natural disasters and deep superstitious fears prevented the ancients from building a third temple on the same site. When they decided, therefore, to erect the new temple (about 370 - 360 B.C.), they had no choice but the west end of the sanctuary, since the area

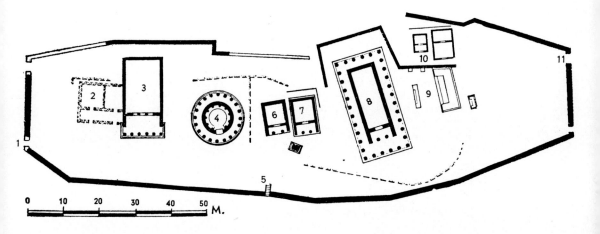

SANCTUARY OF ATHENA PRONAIA

1. *Entrance to the temenos (from the west).*
2. *A 5th century B.C. building, used by the body of priests.*
3. *Later temple of Athena Pronaia, built of stone.*
4. *Tholos.*
5. *Stairway leading through the enclosure into the* temenos.
6. *The so-called Treasury of Massa-*
lia.
7. *Doric treasury.*
8. *Archaic temple of Athena Pronaia, built of poros.*
9. *Levelled area with altars.*
10. *Temple-shaped buildings, possibly belonging to the temenos of the hero Phylakos.*
11. *Entrance to the* temenos *(from the east).*

next to the second temple was occupied by two small Ionic treasuries and the *Tholos* (fig. 3) that had been meanwhile built westwards of the temple. The third temple of Athena, also of the Doric order, had strict geometric proportions and a simple austerity. It had no *pteron,* but only 6 columns in front of the small *pronaos,* and was entirely built of "the most beautiful and most difficult stone to have been used in Delphi: the hard, grey limestone of Mount Parnassos". Its proportions (11 × 22 m.) gave the edifice a particularly serene and classic aspect, and the two Ionic columns, which marked the passage from the front porch to the cella, were the only refinement of the unadorned and pure stone structure.

Between the two ends of the sacred precinct, i.e. between the Archaic and the Classical temple of Athena, there stood in antiquity three exquisite buildings, characterized by the Greek archaeologist and scholar Christos Karouzos as "precious ornaments". First from the east are two small buildings of the "treasury" type. The larger (the eastern one) is of the Doric order and appears to have been built immediately after the Persian Wars (480 - 470

13

B.C.). The smaller, which is of earlier date (530 B.C.), is one of the finest examples of Ionic architecture in the Archaic period, as is the contemporary treasury of the Siphnians in the sanctuary of Apollo. The two columns which supported the architrave in the *pronaos* were Ionic, but had a capital of the curious form that archaeologists have named "Aeolic" — it has a ring of palm leaves curving downwards. Very few remains of the relief decoration have survived. Nevertheless, the glowing Parian marble, which is fashioned with sensitive, masterly skill, particularly at the lower end of the walls where there is a pattern of "spirals" and "astragals", reflects the earlier splendour of this treasury and reveals its beauty, even in the present ruined state.

Between this treasury and the Classical temple of the goddess, stood "the other precious ornament of the sanctuary of Athena, indeed of the whole group of Delphic monuments: the celebrated *"Tholos"*. The purpose of this and other similar *tholoi* in various Greek shrines (Epidauros, Olympia, etc.) is unknown to us, as there is practically no information available on their function. All we can say is that their circular shape derives from a very old tradition and that they are connected with the most sacred cults, probably of a chthonian nature. The Delphic *Tholos* was raised in the early 4th century B.C., on plans by the architect Theodoros. It was entirely built of Pentelic marble in the Doric order, and had a *pteron* of 20 Doric columns. The wall of the cella rests on a layer of dark Eleusinian marble and terminates above into triglyphs and metopes. In the interior of the cella, the floor was paved with schist, and the wall had along its base a moulded podium of Eleusinian marble which supported 10 Corinthian engaged columns. These variations of material, colour and style, and the contrast between the vertical axes of the columns and the curved lines of the *diazoma*, compose an admirable whole. The severe architectural grace of the edifice is enriched by the sculptural decoration of the metopes and produces a delightful impression on the onlooker.

The Sanctuary of Apollo

Leaving the sanctuary of Athena Pronaia behind us, and before reaching the cleft of the Phaidriades, we see on our left the *Gymnasion* as it was modelled in the 4th century B.C. The formation of the ground divides the area into two long and narrow levels. The lower level is smaller. To the east was the *palaistra,* with a central court surrounded by colonnades and rooms behind them, the undressing-room, wrestling-pit, ball-courts, etc. To the west was a large court with a circular basin which served as swimming-pool. After exercising, the youths washed themselves under the spouts in the retaining-wall of the upper terrace and then swam in the cold water. The larger, upper terrace included the *xystos,* a 200 m. long, covered colonnade, where the athletes ran when it was raining, and the *paradromis,* a parallel track in the open air, where they practised in fine weather. The area and facilities of the *Gymnasion* were used not only for physical exercise, but also for lessons, poetry recitals and every kind of cultural activity, as was the case with all the *gymnasia* in ancient Greece.

We continue on our way westwards. To the right is the awe-inspiring gorge, from which emerges the limpid sound of the sacred Kastalian Spring; Apollo's waters flow down generously into the rich green valley. The two great rocks of the Paidriades, Flempoukos to the east and Rhodini to the

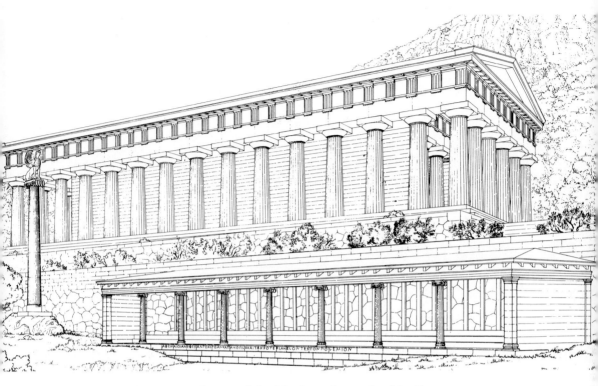

The sphinx of the Naxians, the stoa of the Athenians, the temple of Apollo — reconstruction P. Amandry.

west, tower above us forbiddingly, and seem to touch the sky. And opposite, at the foot of Rhodini, extends the great Delphic sanctuary, the *temenos* of Apollo. Surrounded by a built enclosure, it clings to the slope, occupying an almost rectangular space with a particularly narrow and irregular south side. The main entrance, used by the pilgrims of antiquity, and the visitors of today, is on the southeast corner of the site. In the days of its glory, the holy site must have been the most impressive museum in the world. Elegant edifices, porticoes, official buildings, scattered in a disorderly pattern over the uneven mountain slope, huddling as best as they could to the right and left of the Sacred Way, some of them in a privileged position right by the road-side, others crowding behind, half-hidden, but all of them without exception fashioned with absolute faith in the master of the sanctuary, Apollo Phoibos. And among these buildings, thousands of statues and votive offerings, apart from the more precious ones which were kept in safety within the small, temple-shaped treasuries, as they were called. It would be difficult and tedious to enumerate here all the ruins and bases of monuments, in the order they occur as the visitor proceeds along the Sacred Way from the entrance towards the temple of Apollo. The careful reconstruction by the painter K. Eliakis and the accompanying annotation will permit readers and visitors to form a mental picture of the shrine as it was in antiquity and to identify the ruins of the respective monuments. It would be worthwhile, however, to mention briefly the dedicatory offerings which stood near the entrance to the

15

sacred precinct. The first base to the right was surmounted by the statue of a bull, dedicated to Apollo by the Korkyraians (circa 480 B.C.). Oposite this offering, stood the first large statuary group, a dedication of the Athenians to commemorate their victory at Marathon. This work must have been made about 460 B.C., by the still young Pheidias, and was composed of 13 bronze statues representing Miltiades and ten mythical heroes of Athens, flanked by the divine figures of Athena and Apollo. The Athenians had barely set up their splendid dedication, when their friends, the Argives, hastened to offer their own tanksgiving to the god for their victory over the Spartans at Oinoe in Argolis (456 B.C.), and erected two groups of statues, both on the left-hand side of the Sacred Way, next to the dedication of the Athenians. The first group represented the "Seven against Thebes", and the second the "Epigones" who avenged the disaster of the Seven by defeating the Thebans. Again, in 414 B.C., following a victory over the Spartans, the Argives set up a classical Wooden Horse on the same site. It was now the Spartans' turn to present their offering. In 405 B.C., they defeated the Athenians at Aigos Potamoi, causing the final dissolution of the Athenian hegemony. With understable pride, therefore, they raised their monument, opposite those of their adversaries. They cut the rock, erected a colonnaded building with 8 columns on the façade, and housed in it 37 bronze statues of their patron gods, of their victorious admiral Lysander crowned by Poseidon, and of the other admirals. The battle of dedications does not end here, however. In 371 B.C., the Spartans suffered a severe defeat at Leuktra, and shortly afterwards (369 B.C.) the Arkadians, together with the Theban general Epameinondas, invaded Lakonia. Proud of their achievement, the Arkadians erected, in front of the Spartan dedication, their own statuary group, composed of 9 bronze statues portraying the god Apollo and their mythical ancestors. In the same year, the Argives retaliated upon their perpetual enemies, the Spartans. Next to Lysander's group and opposite their old offering, they raised a new one, consisting of 20 bronze statues of their mythical heroes.

We have walked no farther than 50 m. within the sacred precinct, and we have already counted — in our imagination — 95 statues on either side of the Sacred Way. It is therefore impossible to continue like this, and, if we are to see all the important relics of the sanctuary, we shall have to hasten our pace. The first ruins to the left belong to the Archaic Treasury or the Sikyonians (500 B.C.). Architectural pieces from older buildings were re-used in the construction of this treasury, including the rectangular sculptured metopes, which date from circa 560 B.C. and are of particular significance for the history of Greek sculpture. Four of these metopes are now fairly well preserved. Next, are the remains of one of the most elegant Ionic treasuries in Delphi: the Treasury of the Siphnians. Built in 525 B.C., it was richly adorned with sculptured decoration. The two columns in front of the entrance were in the form of Korai, usually known as Caryatids. The pediment and frieze were decorated with admirable reliefs, which are now displayed in the Delphi Museum and constitute excellent examples of Archaic sculpture (cf. description below).

At this point the Sacred Way describes a curve and ascends obliquely upwards. Immediately after the curve, on the left, is the Treasury of the Athenians. This is a Doric building, the material of which has largely survived, so that archaeologists were able to restore it entirely supplying only very few additions. (The restoration was made on a grant from the Municipality of Athens, before the Second World War). The pediments and metopes were all decorated with reliefs preserved in sufficiently good condition to permit us to appreciate the Attic sculpture of the late Archaic period (cf. description below). Its precise dating has not been established. Some archaeologists believe that the treasury was built after the battle at Marathon, while others support that it was dedicated by the new Athenian democracy (about 505 - 500 B.C.). The walls of the treasury are covered with inscriptions of later date (3rd century B.C. and later), mostly honorific decrees of Athenians. However, among these inscriptions are two of the most important texts of antiquity: two hymns to Apollo, with the musical notation accompanying the text.

Next to the Treasury of the Athenians lie the ruins of the Delphic *Bouleuterion* (Council House), a rectangular poros building of the Archaic period. Higher up, there is a huge rock, presumably fallen there from the Phaidriades in very ancient times, long before the shrine was given its later arrangement. It was called the "rock of Sibyl", because the ancients believed that the first mythical diviner, who was said to have come from Erythrai in Asia Minor, stood on this rock to prophesy. A little higher, another, levelled rock supported a very tall Ionic column, which was surmounted by the Sphinx of the Naxians (cf. below). In the same area was the shrine of Gaia (Earth) with its spring, which was guarded by Python, the terrible serpent subsequently slain by the new god, Apollo. Further east, in front of the polygonal supporting-wall of the temple terrace, the Athenians erected an elegant Ionic stoa with 8 Ionic columns, to shelter the spoils from their naval victories over the Persians (479 B.C.).

To the right of the Sacred Way, opposite the area with the monuments described above, was a small circular place, the sacred *Halos* (Threshing Floor). Here were celebrated every eight years the *Septeria,* a re-enacting of the holy drama representing the killing of the serpent by the god.

The ruins of many other treasuries have survived in various less prominent parts of the sanctuary. They all bear testimony to the worldwide fame enjoyed by Delphi, where all the Greek cities aspired to present rich offerings and erect sacred buildings. Archaeologists have identified, with a greater or lesser degree of certainty, the treasuries of the Knidians, Kyrenaians, Potidaians, Akanthians and Corinthians, while a number of other treasuries still remain anonymous.

But it is the god's temple that has pride of place in the great sanctuary. Half-way up the slope, there is a large terrace, supported on the south side by a fine polygonal wall which was intended to provide a firm base for the temple's foundations (fig. 8). On the north side, there is a retaining wall whose purpose was to protect the temple from falling rocks. The temple we see at present (fig. 7), erected in the 4th century B.C., is the third to have been built on that site (not including of course the three mythical temples of which the first was said to have been made entirely of laurel leaves, the second of feathers and wax, and the third of bronze). The first temple of Apollo was built in the 7th century B.C. and was destroyed by fire in 548 B.C. It was replaced by the Archaic temple of the Alkmeonidai, which was built with contributions by both Greeks and non-Greeks; it is the temple that displayed on its eastern pediment (made of marble) the god's Epiphany to mankind, when he arrived at Delphi on a chariot with his mother, Leto, and his sister, Artemis. This temple, too, was destroyed, in 373 B.C., and was

Sphinx of the Naxians — reconstruction.

rebuilt between 369 B.C. and 330 B.C., on plans by the architects Spintharos of Corinth, Xenodoros and Agathon. This temple, which was slightly larger than that of the Alkmeonidai (measuring 60.32 × 23.82 m.), was a Doric *peripteros,* with a surrounding colonnade of 6 columns on the ends and 15 at the sides. The east pediment was decorated with the same theme as that of the older temple, while the west pediment depicted the setting of the Sun (Helios), and Dionysos with the Thyiades. With the possible exception of the figure of Dionysos, all the other sculptures have perished. The interior arrangement of the temple poses many questions. The damage in several important parts is such that it has led to the supposition that it had been purposely effected, either by the last of the heathens in order to prevent the Christians from desecrating their holy shrine, or by the Christians out of fanaticism. It is in this temple that the Pythia probably uttered her last oracle, addressed to Emperor Julian, and it was on the walls of the temple's *pronaos* that the visitor read those famous engraved proverbs "nothing in excess" and "know thyself", and the mysterious Delphic letter E, the secret significance of which neither the ancient Greeks nor modern scholars have been able to discover. And finally, it was in this temple, as in the ones that preceded it, that the Delphic oracle was sheltered: the *adyton,* with the oracular tripod and next to it the *omphalos,* which the ancient Greeks believed to be the tomb of Python. Not far from these ran the waters of the Kassotis Spring. All this information has been obtained from ancient writers. Excavations have not been able to throw additional light on the matter, because the destruction of relevant data was total; even the position and form of the *adyton* cannot be reconstructed with certainty.

To the north of the temple, on the northwest corner of the sanctuary, lies the theatre (fig. 16), and east of that the famous *Lesche* (club) of the Knidians, where the great artist Polygnotos painted the sack of Troy and Odysseus' descent into Hades. Finally, at the highest point outside the sanctuary was the Delphic *stadion* (fig. 10), where the Pythian Games were held. Pindar celebrated these Games in his fine triumphal odes to the *Pythionikai* (Pythian victors), the most famous among whom were Hieron of Syracuse and Arkesilaos of Kyrene.

The visitor who wishes to experience to the full the beauty of the Delphic site and fill his spirit with the unique vision of its landscape and monuments will discover, as he wanders slowly and reverently through the ruins, the pedestals of celebrated offerings and will read their fine inscriptions: "The Chians dedicated the altar to Apollo" reads the 5th century B.C. inscription on the monumental altar standing at the entrance to the temple, where the preliminary sacrifice to the god was offered (figs. 14 and 7). At a small distance, we find a plain uninscribed pedestal, which was surmounted by the gold tripod offered to the sanctuary by 31 Greek cities after the victory at Plataia (fig. 14). Higher up the slope, there were four more gold tripods, dedicated by the four sons of Deinomenes: Gelon, Hieron, Polyzalos and Thrasyboulos, after their victory over the Carthaginians in 479 B.C. Still further up, to the north-east of the temple, stood the offering of Daochos, the rich Thessalian who erected a statue of Apollo and eight statues of his ancestors, as well as that of himself and his son; among these, the statue of his great-grandfather, Agias, has survived and is now in the Museum of Delphi (fig. 48). Before we end this rather limited selection of famous votive offerings, we feel bound to remind the reader of one of the finest and most important, historically speaking: namely, the votive offering of Krateros, the celebrated general of Alexander the Great. To the north of the north-west corner of the temple, enclosed within a kind of portico, there were several bronze statues representing Alexander the Great and Krateros engaged in a lion-hunt; this offering was the work of two eminent sculptors of that period (320 B.C.), Lysippos and Leochares.

The excavations

In the centuries that followed the closing-down of the oracle, the site was stripped of all the invaluable works of art which had survived the repeated plunder of the emperors. As time went by, the buildings gradually fell into ruin and were covered with a thick layer of soil, which only just allowed some piece of marble, some faint inscription to appear here and there. Then there came a time when a tiny village, Kastri, was built on the site where the old sanctuary had once stood. In 1892, when the French Archaeological

School began excavating the site, the entire village was expropriated by the Greek government and removed to its present position. The French archaeologists uncovered the whole sacred site; their excavations brought to light Apollo's sanctuary and revealed to our bedazzled eyes, the most sacred monuments of the ancient Greek world. The works of art that had escaped destruction, however few, suddenly spoke to us in their own divine fashion about their lost gods.

THE MUSEUM: Kleobis and Biton

The Museum of Delphi, built in 1902, rebuilt in 1937-1938 and repaired after the war, shelters masterpieces of an artistic Amphiktyony, as it were, that had sent its representative works from every corner of the Greek land and from every period of Greek history.

First among the cities represented here is Argos. In the dawn of the Archaic age, Argos sent its offering to the god; it is the first exhibit to be seen in the Museum of Delphi. The dedication consisted of the statues of two Argive youths, Kleobis and Biton, who harnessed themselves to their mother's chariot and drove her from the city of Argos to the sanctuary of Hera, i.e. a distance of no less than 45 stadia (8 klm.). Everybody marvelled at her good fortune in having two such sons; and the proud mother prayed to the goddess and begged her to bestow upon her sons the greatest blessing men dare hope for. Then all three offered sacrifice, ate their supper and went to sleep in the sanctuary. But Kleobis and Biton never woke again. The goddess had granted their mother's wish. It was the statues of these two youths that the Argives set up in the sanctuary of Delphi, as Herodotos recounts. Their physical vigour enabled them to gain immortality. In these two Archaic Kouroi Polymedes has admirably rendered the sense of physical strength, of athletic fitness; there is the sturdy modelling of the bodies, the broad chests and narrow waists, the powerful muscles, the square heads, the sharp emphasis on the articulations which both join and separate the various parts of the anatomy (fig. 18).

A few years later (560 B.C.), Naxos, a prosperous Cycladic island, also sent a votive offering to the Delphic god; it is the famous Naxian Sphinx, whose exquisite figure towers above a tall column 9.32 metres high (fig. 24). This daemonic creature, with its powerful form fascinated Greek artists, especially in the Archaic age. The Naxians' offering presents us with one of the earliest examples of this mythical figure. However, the craftsmen of Archaic Greece had already covered much ground by the time they reached this level of artistic achievement. The rhythmical juxtaposition of curves betrays a wealth of experience and a highly cultivated sensitivity; the large wide-open eyes, the tight lips convey a fascinating unwordly expression; the brilliant side-view reveals the artist's skill and audacity. The whole work testifies to the piety and wealth of the Naxians in the early Archaic period.

The metopes of the Treasury of the Sikyonians

Other even wealthier cities raised whole edifices — the famous "treasuries" — to honour the god and display their own power and piety. In these buildings, sculptural decoration competed with, and sometimes surpassed, architectural beauty. The city of Sikyon, rich and powerful in Archaic

The Treasury of the Siphnians — reconstruction, A. Tournaire. Principal façade.

times, raised its treasury around 560 B.C. at the beginning of the Sacred Way. It seems that this edifice presented many unusual features (it was later replaced by another building). One of its singularities was that the metopes did not have the customary square shape, but were rectangular, as we can see in the surviving pieces exhibited in the Museum of Delphi. One of the metopes (fig. 19) represents the Dioskouroi, Kastor and Polydeukes, and the Apharidai, Idas and Lyngeus, following each other in an impressive formation; in between, we can see the heads of the oxen which they had stolen in the course of some joint raid — probably the one that ended with the murder of Kastor and the Apharidai. The artist illustrates the myth with remarkable order and clarity; he has even added the characters' names next to their figures, so that the spectator shall be in no doubt about their identity. Another metope, much more audacius both in conception and execution, represents the mythical ship, Argo, beaching upon the distant shores of Kolchis. In both

The Treasury of the Siphnians — reconstruction A. Tournaire.

these metopes, the dominant intention is to depict clear, solid figures in the plenitude of their motionless presence. A third metope, representing the rape of Europe by Zeus who had assumed the form of a bull, and a fourth, representing the wild boar in the celebrated Kalydonian hunt, convey impetuous movement in the most convincing manner.

The Siphnian Treasury

Next to the Treasury of Sikyon, the Siphnians erected their own treasury in the year 525 B.C. The small Cycladic island of Siphnos, lived in great prosperity in those distant times, drawing immeasurable wealth from its gold and silver mines. Herodotos considered Siphnos as "one of the richest islands". Its inhabitants, therefore, aspired to dedicate to Apollo a votive offering that would be unique both in beauty and opulence. The Siphnian treasury was not very large (8.55×6.12 metres), but it was built entirely of glowing Parian marble: the first edifice in mainland Greece to be built wholly in marble. However, it was not the building itself that acquired fame in ancient Greece or that moves us most today, but its magnificent ornamentation. The predominance of sculpture over architecture reaches its highest peak in the Treasury of the Siphnians; statues were even used in place of main architectural parts. For instance, between the two antae, instead of Ionic columns there were two Korai supporting the architrave (fig. 23), a solution that was later to be put to brilliant use in the Erechtheion. The Korai stand upon high pedestals and are shown in sumptuous Ionic attire and jewellery. The artist has managed to maintain the self-sufficiency of these auxiliary figures without neglecting their fundamentally architectural function. Perhaps no other work of art can help us appreciate so clearly the ability of the Archaic sculptors, the sureness and confidence with which they fashioned any form they wished, always remaining keenly aware of both the requirements of their art and the functional demands of their work.

Pedimental sculptures of the Siphnian Treasury

Above the architrave, the building is adorned on all four sides by a splendid frieze, the most exquisite in the Archaic period, a remote forerunner of the Classical frieze of the Parthenon. The east pediment at the back of the treasury has retained its sculptures, depicting a charming and typical myth related to Delphi, a favourite theme to both sculptors and vase-painters in the late Archaic period. Herakles, frantic with remorse for having murdered Iphitos, consulted the Delphic oracle about how he should cleanse himself. The Pythia would not answer him, because he was still defiled with the blood he had shed: upon which the son of Zeus snatched away the oracular tripod and prepared to leave. But Apollo also a son a Zeus and master of the oracle, could not remain indifferent to Herakles' action; he tried to take the tripod back. The carving on the pediment depicts the very moment when Athena intervenes and takes the two opponents by the hand in order to stop them from fighting each other (fig. 25).

The frieze of the Siphnian Treasury

The most exquisite feature of the edifice, though, is the frieze. On the west side, it depicts the judgement of Paris, on the south the rape of the Leukippidai by the Dioskouroi, on the east an assembly of gods (fig. 26), who watch a battle of the Trojan War (fig. 27), and on the north which is the finest and best preserved section of the entire frieze, the Gigantomachy (figs. 28-30). Here we see the gods fighting hard to defeat the Giants, who are attacking from the right, wearing heavy armoury: helmets and shields, and in some cases breastplates and greaves; their weapons are spears, swords and stones. The left section of the frieze is taken up by the gods. On the extreme left, Hephaistos, wearing the short *chiton* of a craftsman, is shown standing in front of his fellows and preparing his redhot bolts. Next come two goddesses, Demeter and Kore; then Dionysos, wearing a panther skin, and Kybele riding a chariot drawn by lions (fig. 29). Then come Leto's beloved children, Apollo and Artemis, shooting arrows at their opponents; they are facing a warrior with a *kantharos* on his helmet: he is the Giant Kantharos (fig. 30). The next section of the frieze which has been damaged, showed Zeus riding his chariot. Hera and Athena have survived, in a good state of preservation; next to them Ares is wearing a helmet and holding a shield; Hermes follows, wearing the conical cap of Arkadian shepherds (fig. 28); finally, come Poseidon and Amphitrite, but only fragments of the lower part of their bodies have survived.

The sculptor who produced the Gigantomachy and the battle between the Greeks and the Trojans must have been one of the great artists of his age, endowed with a powerful and daring imagination, unique technical skill and a deep awareness of the difficulties of relief sculpture. It is enough to notice the extraordinary rendering of the successive surfaces of the figures, which though frequently intertwined, always remain clearly distinct from each other. The impetus of the conflict and the mingling of the adversaries is reproduced with great power and intensity, without however damaging the clarity of form and the easy, flowing rhythm which carries us from left to right and back again, with admirable skill, in a movement not unlike the ebb and flow of a wave. But apart from its power and robust expressiveness, the frieze retains its decorative character; it is a sensitive arrangement and exploitation of a surface demanding to be filled, an impressive, but also festive development of the theme, with all the spiritual exaltation appropriate to the sacred site of Delphi.

The Treasury of the Athenians

There is a third treasury, which has survived in a fairly good condition and has been restored *in situ* with very few additions: it is the treasury which the Athenians dedicated to the sanctuary during the last years of the 6th century B.C., soon after the establishment of democracy in their city (508 B.C.). Only a few fragments remain from the pediments; but of the metopes there are enough left to enable us to reconstruct their themes almost in their entirety (figs. 32-33). On the main sections — i.e., the façade and the south side, which was more exposed to public view, there are representations of the exploits of Theseus, whom the Athenians regarded as the legendary founder of democracy; at the back of the treasury and on the north side we see the labours of Herakles. These reliefs are a good example of Attic sculpture during the last phase of the Archaic period, and they bring to the spectator's mind the early, red-figured vase-paintings of that time, with their elegant figures, lightly-balanced proportions, firm and spirited movement, daring postures, flexible contours, careful and thoroughly studied rendering of muscles and draperies.

The Charioteer

The tyrants of Syracuse, the famous sons of Deinomenes, were wealthy, ambitious and much interested in the arts. They set up golden tripods at Delphi after the battle of Imera (479 B.C.); they also sent their chariots to win laurel crowns at the great pan-Hellenic games, and commissioned great poets like Pindar or Bakchylides to sing their victories. One of them, Polyzalos,

Treasury of the Athenians — reconstruction A. Tournaire.

"king of Gela", won the chariot-race at the Pythian Games of 478 B.C. He then sent a magnificent votive offering to the sanctuary of the Pythian Apollo: a bronze chariot drawn by four horses and driven by a charioteer. The earthquake of 373 B.C. dislodged huge rocks from the mountain-side, destroying the temple and several other edifices and votive offerings, among which Polyzalos' splendid gift. However, fortune proved relatively kind: the

Treasury of the Athenians — reconstruction A. Tournaire, principal façade.

Charioteer was saved, practically intact, and Delphi reverently buried him
when the site was levelled down for the construction of the new temple. That
is how the magnificent Charioteer has reached us and taken its place as the
most prized exhibit in the Museum of Delphi (figs. 45-46).

The young man, whom we call the Charioteer, stands upright, his two
bare feet well planted on the chariot, proudly carrying his tall frame (1.80
metres), his hands (only the right one has been preserved) loosely holding the
reins. He is wearing the long robe of a charioteer, secured tightly under the
armpits by the *analabos,* to stop it from fluttering in the strong wind as he
races along on his chariot; the victor's band (made of silver and inlaid) is tied
on his brow; his gaze is fixed ahead, luminous but betraying a slight fatigue
due to the excitement of the race. His stature, the structure of his tall and
slender body, the arrangement of the folds in his robe, the firm position of his
bare feet, the sense of strength combined with ease conveyed by his right

hand holding the reins, the tiny, imperceptible movements, the subtle divergences from a strictly frontal position, the secret signs of a pulsating inner life — all this, accomplished with the help of innumerable details and in a manner that has remained quite unique, give the Charioteer of Delphi a monumental impressiveness and at the same time the glow of a living creature. The firm structure of the body is crowned by that unique head, with its extraordinary clarity of form, with the exquisite tracery of the hair, the intelligent gaze, the fleshy lips and cheeks, all powerfully framing the inner bone structure. The strength and fascination conveyed by every great work of art are successfully combined in this masterpiece with a noble gracefulness and a style that is both severe and joyful, so that the spectator is carried back in time to that triumphant moment when the victorious charioteer, proud and self-controlled at the same time, receives the crowd's applause as if it were an additional laurel wreath.

Innumerable masterpieces of this class filled the sacred site of Delphi in those distant times. Not long after the Charioteer, the Athenians sent their own magnificent offering, a "tithe" from the battle of Marathon: 13 bronze statues by the hand of Pheidias. The Argives, and then the Lakedaimonians and the Arkadians also sent votive offerings; upon first setting foot on the Sacred Way, the pilgrims were surrounded by a multitude of bronze statues; about a hundred different figures of gods and heroes welcomed them, bringing word that in this sanctuary friends and enemies could happily coexist, under the protection of Apollo, the radiant god of all the Hellenes.

The votive offering of Daochos

All this is now lost forever. But in the Museum of Delphi, we can still see whatever remains from another offering of the late 4th century B.C. Although it cannot be compared to the splendid monuments presented by the proud Greek cities, the votive offering of the Thessalian Daochos, who represented his country at the Delphic Amphiktyony from 338 to 334 B.C., gives an unmistakable impression of opulence. It consisted of a large pedestal (which has survived) upon which stood Daochos himself with his son and his forefathers, five generations in all, facing Apollo's statue. Enough remains of these men's bodies to gain a fairly accurate estimate of this work's value. One of the best preserved figures among them is Agias, Daochos' great-grandfather, an athlete who had won considerable fame in the middle of the 5th century B.C. He won an Olympic victory in the *pankration* contest and was five times victor of the Nemean Games, three times of the Pythian Games and five times of the Isthmian Games. This is then the legendary figure represented by the young athlete standing today in the Museum of Delphi, with his sinewy body, his bent elbows and weary head (fig. 48). The structure of the naked body, made up of a multitude of expressive, counter-balancing movements, the modelling of masses, the powerful proportions, these all embody the artistic *credo* prevailing in the late 4th century B.C. There can be no doubt that this is the work of a major artist. We also know that a bronze statue of this athlete was set up at Pharsalos, with the inscription: "this is the work of Lysippos of Sikyon". It is highly probable, therefore, that the marble statue at Delphi was a contemporary copy of the Pharsalos statue, and that it was made with the approval of the great sculptor, to say the least, if not in his own workshop.

The "dancers"

The dedicant of the elaborate and unusual offering known as the "column with the dancers" (fig. 47) has remained unknown to this day. A tall, slender column ll metres high is entwined at the base with acanthus leaves; other leaves seem to grow out of the column's trunk at intervals. Three maidens, their backs leaning against the top of the column, lead a light and graceful dance all around it, like flowers growing among the thick foliage of this strange plant. It is impossible for us to say who were these exotic figures with their short tunics and high headdresses. They have been called Graces, then thought to be Thyadai, i.e. Maenads (dancers of Dionysos); they have even been described as Karyatids, i.e. Lakonian girls dancing. Whatever they may be, their dance is undoubtedly sacred, dedicated to the god for his own enjoyment together with the votive offering set up in the Delphic *temenos*.

Hellenistic and Roman votive offerings

From the remaining exhibits at the Museum of Delphi, the visitor will surely single out a remarkable early Hellenistic statue representing a philosopher (fig. 49). There is also a portrait head, the beard beautifully and precisely rendered, the features sharp and alien-looking (fig. 50). Whether it portrays some Macedonian prince or some Hellenized personage from the East, or whether it is, as some archaeologists suggest, a portrait of the Roman Flamininus, this fine head certainly gives an idea of how much Hellenistic art had to offer at its peak years in the field of portraiture.

Finally we come to the statue of Antinoos (fig. 51). When Apollo's priest, Aristotimos, set it up in the sanctuary, the radiant god of Delphi may have considered it a provocation or he may have delighted in the presence of this beautiful boy. It is rather improbable that the priest of the Pythian Apollo should have thought it irreverent to present this enchanting youth to his god. For all we know, the priest may well have believed in Emperor Hadrian's command, proclaiming his beloved youth a god after his death. All we can say at present is that the gentle figure, meditating nostalgically upon a glorious past, closes the long series of votive offerings on a note of tenderness and serenity. It is obvious that by that time the last spark of inner energy and ardour has died away, that the oil in the lamp of the ancient world is running low, and that men sadly contemplate the abandonment of their old ideals. Antinoos is a noble, though languid and lifeless figure, which eloquently shows what remains of plastic form when it lacks inner force, the vigorous manly spirit which gave life to the glorious athletic youths of Greek sculpture.

Column with the dancing girls — reconstruction.

1. Paved court and stoa in front of the main entrance.
2. Bull of Korkyra.
3. Bronze statues dedicated by the Arkadians.
4. Base of the statue of Philopoimen.
5. Bases of votive offerings.
6. Building with stoa, a dedication of the Spartans to commemorate their victory at Aigos Potamoi.
6A. Most likely position of the 37 or 38 classical bronze statues of the Spartans, their offering for the victory at Aigos Potamoi.
7. Wooden Horse of Argos.
8. Dedication of the Athenians to commemorate their victory at Marathon.
9. Statues of the "Seven against Thebes", dedicated by the Argives.
10. Statues of the "Epigones", dedicated by the Argives.
11. Statues of mythical heroes, an offering of Argos.
12. 13, 14. Niches which held votive offerings.
15. Bronze statues of horses and captives, an offering of the Tarentines.
16. Treasury of the Sikyonians.
17. Treasury of the Siphnians.
18. Treasury of the Megarians.
19. Treasury of the Syracusans.
20. Treasury of the Knidians.
21. Aiolian treasury.
22. Offerings of the Aitolians.
23. Treasury of the Thebans.
24. Poros treasury of the Boiotians.
25. Treasury of the Poteidaians.
26. Treasury of the Athenians.
27. The Delphic Bouleuterion (Council House).
28. Archaic treasury in the Asklepieion.
29. Rock of Sibyl.
30. Sphinx of the Naxians.
31. Rock of Leto.
32. Base of a Boiotian offering.
33. Stoa of the Athenians.
34. Treasury of the Corinthians.
35. Treasury of Kyrene.
36. Building assumed to be the Delphic Prytaneion (Magistrates' Hall).
37. Treasury of the Akanthians and Brasidas.
38. Chariot of Helios, dedicated by the Rhodians.
39. Tripod of Plataia.
40. Altar of Apollo, dedicated by the Chians.
41. Statue of Aemilius Paulus.
42. Statue of Apollo Sitalkas.
43. Tripods offered by the Deinomenidai.
44. Archaic treasury.
45. Statue of Attalos I.
46. Statue of Eumenes II.
47. Stoa of Attalos I.
48. The column with the three female dancers.
49. Offering of Daochos.
50. Lesche of the Knidians.
51. Temple of Apollo.
52. Two treasuries.
53. Theatre.
54. Stoa outside the enclosure, accessible from the rear porch of the great temple.

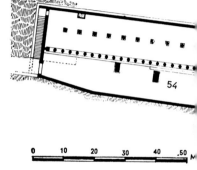

54

0   10   20   30   40   .50   M

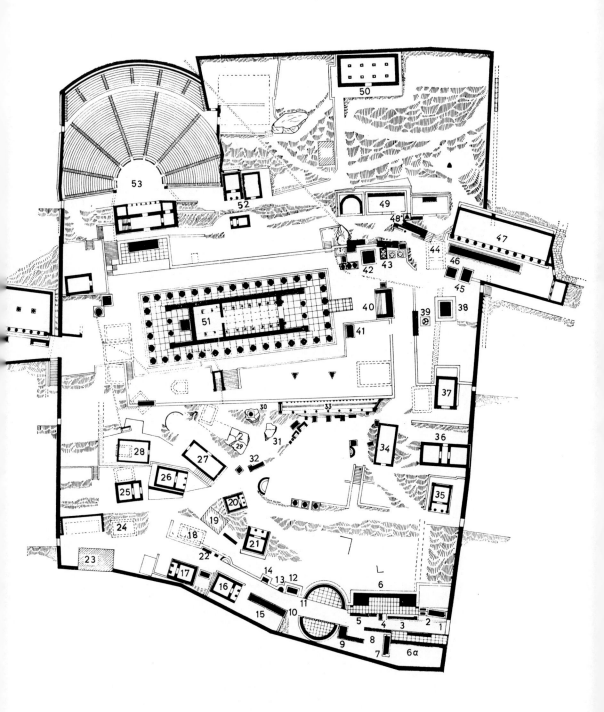

1. The Treasury of the Athenians. It was dedicated to the sanctuary of Delphi immediately after the establishment of democracy in Athens (508 B.C.). The treasury is shown here from the south-east side, which is exactly how it appears to the modern visitor coming up the Sacred Way.

1

2. General view of the site of Delphi, believed in antiquity to be the centre of the earth. One can see the deep valley of the Pleistos river, the fertile plain of Krisa, and in the background the gulf of Itea. The modern road passing in front of the Museum is visible at the centre of the picture. On the slope of Rhodini lie the ruins of the sanctuary of Apollo, with the theatre and the stadion further up the hill.

3. The sanctuary of Athena Pronaia (Marmaria) includes one of the masterpieces of ancient Greek architecture: the Tholos. It is a circular building of the Doric order with well-balanced proportions and finely wrought details. The edifice was of special importance, but its function has remained unknown to this day. c. 380 B.C.

4. View of the tholos *from the east. The three Doric columns of the* pteron *are restored. The entablature has triglyphs and metopes decorated in relief (Battle of the Amazons).*

5. View of the temenos of Athena Pronaia from the east, showing the tholos *and the ruins of two of the treasuries.*

5

6. *General view of the Delphic sanctuary, seen from the Phaidriades. Following the Sacred Way (below left), the visitor of ancient times found himself surrounded by treasuries and offerings, and ended up at the temple of Apollo, where the oracles were delivered. The Pythian festival included pan-Hellenic musical and gymnastic contests held at the stadion (top right).*

7. *The great temple of Apollo, the most important building in the sanctuary, was the centre of the god's cult and oracle. The ruins had belonged to the 4th century B.C. temple. On the right, the tall pedestal of the monument of Prusias.*

7

8. This fine, polygonal wall was built after the fire of 548 B.C. in order to retain the terrace on which the temple stood. The columns belong to the stoa, built by the Athenians after 478 B.C. to shelter spoils of war dedicated to the god after their victories at sea.

9. A section of the Sacred Way which lies before the stoa and the Treasury of the Athenians.

10. A view of the stadion of Delphi (5th century B.C.). The rows of seats, made of Parnassian stone, are of the Roman age.

11. *The sacred spring of Kastalia, inseparably associated with the oracle and the cult of Apollo in general, issues between the two rocks known as the Phaidriades. The fountain as it now appears dates from the Hellenistic and Roman times.*

12. *The sacred spring of Kastalia as it is today. It dates from the Archaic and Classical periods.*

13. *View of the north stoa of the Roman agora, with a row of shops at the back of it. The agora was built in the 4th century A.D.*

1

13

14. *The terminal point of the Sacred Way, just before the temple. On the right, the large 5th century B.C. altar presented by the Chians. On the left, the circular stone base of the votive tripod offered by the Greek cities for their victory at Plataia, one of the most important monuments of Greek history.*

15. *Doric columns of poros from the* pteron *of the temple of Apollo.*

15

16. *The well-preserved theatre of Delphi, built of Parnassian limestone, stands at the north-west corner of the sacred precinct. Its position, high up on the slope, affords a unique view of the Delphic landscape.*

17. *Hellenistic or Roman copy of the Archaic omphalos (navel-stone). It is covered by the agrenon, a kind of thick net, and was surmounted by the two golden eagles of Zeus that flew from the two ends of the world to meet at its centre, at Delphi.*

16   17

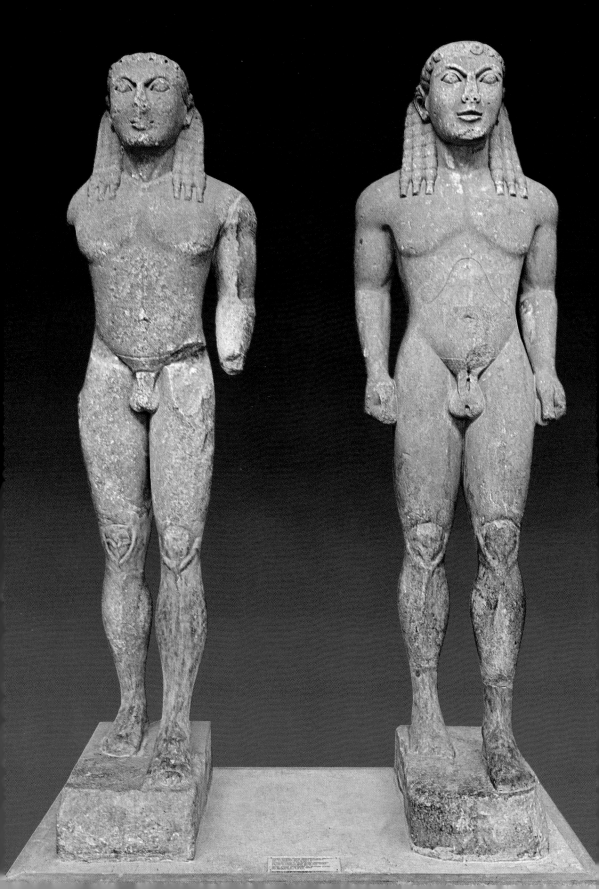

18. *Kleobis and Biton. This group of the two Kouroi was dedicated to the Delphic sanctuary by the Argives in the early 6th century B.C. It is the work of the Argive sculptor (Poly)medes and a good example of the style of this Peloponnesian workshop. The inscription at the base records their achievement and preserves part of the artist's name. c. 590 B.C.*

19. *One of the metopes of the Treasury of the Sikyonians. It represents Kastor, Polydeukes and Idas (followed by Lyngeus on the section now missing). The names of the figures represented are designated by inscriptions, barely legible at present, painted in colour. Armed with spears, they are shown leading away the oxen they had stolen in a joint raid. c. 560 B.C.*

19

20. *Poros metope with a scene of the Calydonian boar. From the Sicyonian Treasury.*

21. *Poros metope with a scene from the expedition of the Argonauts. From the Sicyonian Treasury.*

22. *Flying Nike (Victory); corner akroterion on the façade of the Archaic temple of Apollo. c. 510 B.C.*

23. *Torso of one of the two Korai supporting the entablature of the Siphnian Treasury. These female figures were used instead of columns and became known later as Karyatids. c. 525 B.C.*

22

23

24. The Sphinx of the Naxians. This demonic Sphinx, offered to the sanctuary by the wealthy Naxians, crouched upon a tall Ionic column that stood south of the temple of Apollo, near the Sibyl's rock. The Cycladic island of Naxos possessed considerable riches and power in the Archaic period, and the Naxian workshop of sculpture produced a number of important works of art. c. 560 B.C.

25

26

25. The east pediment of the Siphnian Treasury. It illustrates the myth of the dispute between Herakles and Apollo over the Delphic tripod. In the middle we see Athena intervening between Herakles (on the right) and Apollo (on the left), as they each tug away at the tripod. Artemis is shown behind Apollo trying to support her brother by the arms. c. 525 B.C.

26. Left section of the east frieze of the Siphnian Treasury. The subject here is the assembly of the gods who watch a battle of the Trojan War. The gods shown on this section championed the Trojan camp: Ares, Aphrodite, Artemis, Apollo and Zeus (whose head is missing). c. 525 B.C.

27. *Right section of the east frieze of the Siphnian Treasury. A battle between Greeks and Trojans.*

28. *Right section of the north frieze. From left to right: a Giant, Ares stooping over a dead Giant, two Giants, Hermes wearing his conical cap and two more Giants.*

29, 30. *Left section of the north frieze of the Siphnian Treasury, representing the Gigantomachy. The gods are fighting the Giants, who are shown as hoplites. From left to right: two Giants, Dionysos, Kybele riding a chariot drawn by lions. Fig. 30: Apollo and Artemis, the Giant Kantharos, a dead Giant and three other Giants.*

31. Metope from the south side of the Treasury of the Athenians. It depicts the duel between Theseus and Antiope, queen of the Amazons.

32. Metope from the north side of the Treasury of the Athenians. It shows Herakles overcoming the Kerynitian stag. Dated to c. 500 B.C.

33. Four-horse chariot, from the south frieze of the Siphnian Treasury. This side of the frieze, like the west side, is probably the work of an artist of Ionian origin; both sides are not as well preserved as the rest. A number of horses have survived, either ridden by horsemen or harnessed to chariots. If we compare this artist to the creator of the east and north sections, the artistic excellence of the latter becomes obvious.

33

34. *Ivory carved with relief figures. A warrior is departing in his chariot. Ionian work from the 6th century B.C.*

35. *Carved ivory with female (Harpies) and male (Boreades) figures. Mythological scene. From a Corinthian workshop. c. 570 B.C.*

35

36. Male head (Apollo?) of ivory, from a gold and ivory statue of a figure seated on a throne. There is a gilded silver plate on the head, and two large gold curls of hair on the breast. Ionian work of the 6th century B.C., dedicated to Apollo.

37. Female head of ivory — probably the goddess Artemis. She wears a gold diadem. Ionian dedication from the 6th century B.C.

38. Two semi-circular gold plates supported on bronze plaques with Gorgons. c. 560 B.C.

39. Square gold plate supported on a bronze plaque with a griffin carved in relief. c. 560 B.C.

39

40-41. Gold plates, which were used to decorate the dress of a gold and ivory statue. (Fig. 36). The upper and lower edges have a band of relief

41

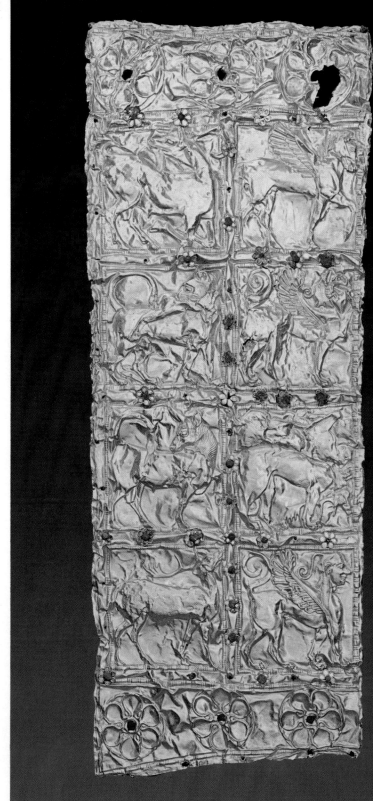

rosettes, and the rest of the surface is decorated with relief animals in squares separated by bands. From an Ionian workshop. c. 560 B.C.

42. *Gold diadems.*

43. *Two gold volutes from the leg of a throne that belonged to the seated gold and ivory statue.*

42

44. *Gold flowers with four sepals and four stamens, made in three separate sections.*

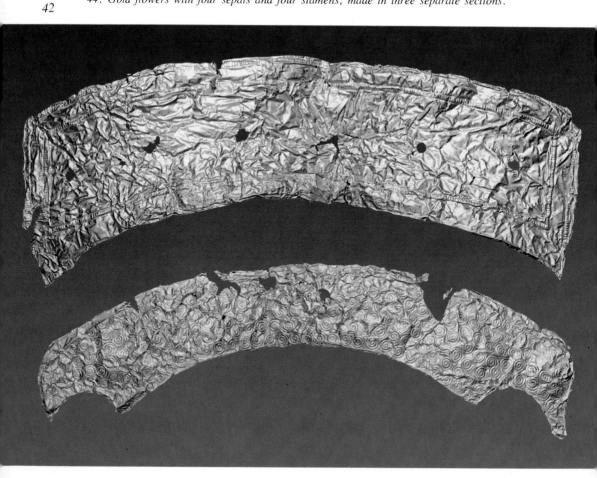

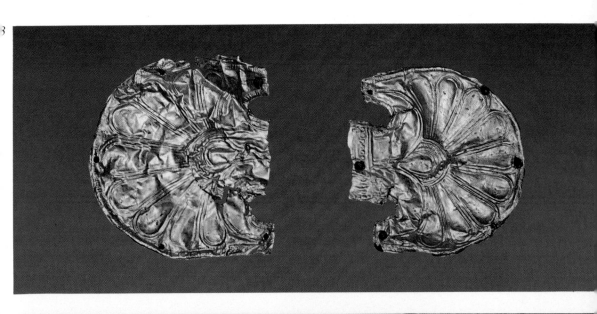

45

45-46. The Charioteer is one of the finest products of the 'severe style'. He was found practically intact; the composition included a bronze chariot drawn by four horses. It was dedicated to the sanctuary by Polyzalos, tyrant of Gela, around 475 B.C., following his victory at the Pythian Games.

47. One of the most at-
tractive and enigmatic
monuments found at
Delphi is this column
with the three female
dancers. The entire
monument must have
been about 13 m. high; it
consisted of a column en-
circled with acanthus
leaves; at the top, three
maidens, wearing the
sacred headgear, are
engaged in what is obvi-
ously a ritual dance. The
column was surmounted
by a tripod. The dedicant
of this offering is un-
known. All we can say is
that this is a work by an
Ionian artist of the early
4th century B.C.

48. The statue of Agias
was one of a group of
nine dedicated by the
Thessalian Daochos; it
comes from the workshop
of Lysippos, the great
Sikyonian sculptor of the
second half of the 4th
century B.C.

49. Statue of a philo-
sopher. It is a remarka-
ble work, typical of the
early Hellenistic period
and possibly a product of
the Attic workshop. c.
250 B.C.

47

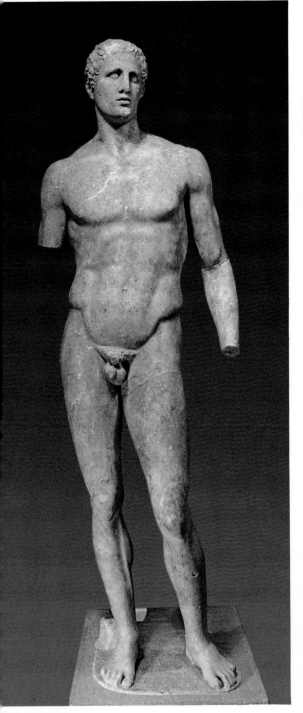

48

49

50. This fine portrait occupies pride of place in the art of portraiture of the mature Hellenistic period (first half of the 2nd century B.C.). The forceful plastic modelling, the expressive intensity of the face combine to produce a composition which represents Hellenistic art at its best. Some archaeologists regard it as a portrait of Flamininus, the Roman general who defeated Philip V in 197 B.C. at Kynos Kephalai.

51. The statue of Antinoos at Delphi is one of the finest portraits of this lovely youth. After his death, Emperor Hadrian, who loved him passionately, proclaimed him a god and ordered his statue to be set up in innumerable cities throughout the Roman empire. This graceful, melancholy figure, which reflects the world of the Imperial age, embodying the external strength and aesthetic passion that tempted to conceal the decay and decline of the ancient world, was encountered in the remotest regions of the Mediterranean, from Africa to Greece, from Syria to Western Europe. A.D. 130-138.

51

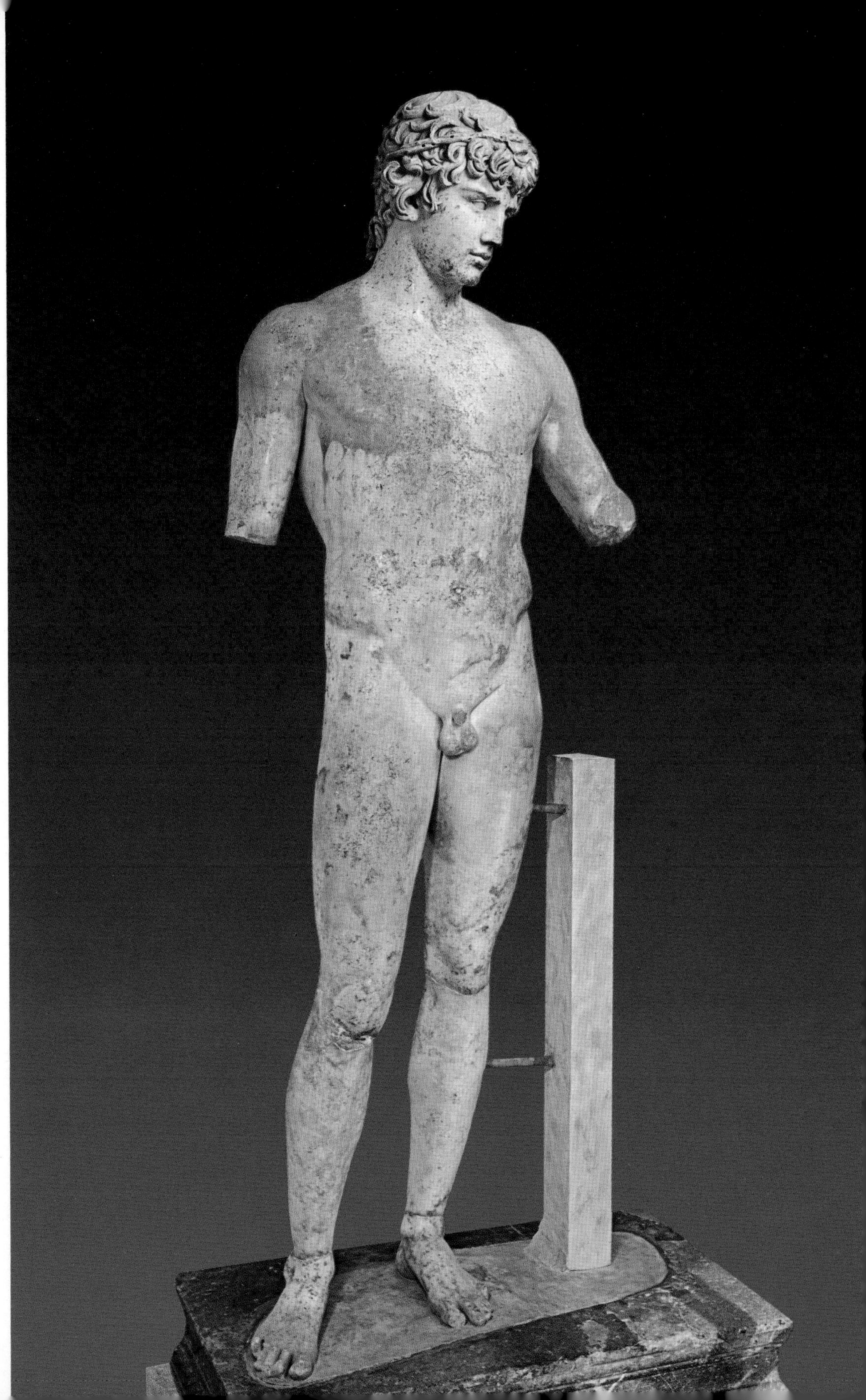

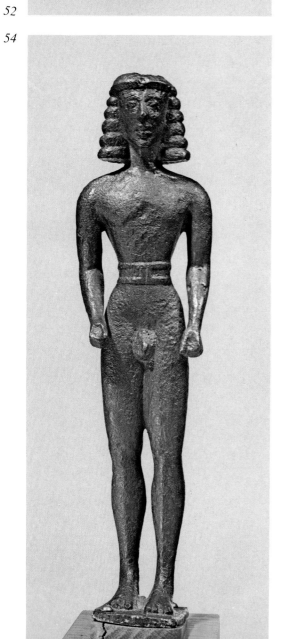

52. *Head of a griffin adorning a bronze tripod. 7th century B.C.*

53. *Composition representing Odysseus (or one of his companions) clinging to the belly of a ram in order to escape unnoticed from the cave of the Cyclop Polyphemos. This was part of the ornamenation on an early Archaic bronze tripod.*

54. *This very early bronze Kouros from Delphi is an exceptionally fine example of 'Daidalic art'; it transcends the limitations of its small size and produces a monumental effect. Mid.-7th century B.C.*

55. *Bronze figurine probably representing Apollo c. 525 B.C.*

56. *Bronze censer; the peplos-clad female figure holds a semi-spherical vessel in her raised hands. c. 450 B.C.*

56

57. *Apollo pouring libations. Interior of a white kylix found at Delphi. Apollo is seated, with great poise and majesty, upon a folding diphros (stool). His garment is unusual for a male figure: he is wearing a peplos and a himation. In his left hand he holds his lyre and with his right he pours the libation from a phiale. On the left-hand side of the composition a bird is perched on a wooden bar; this may be Apollo's sacred bird, the raven, or (more likely) a wild dove, like those that come to roost in his temple. There is a divine nobility and a profound spirituality about this beautiful, laurel-crowned head with its finely dressed hair. The precision and flowing ease of the design, the colour harmony and the architectural solidity of the whole composition indicate that this vase must have been painted by one of the finest artists in the early years of the 'severe style'. c. 470 B.C.*

57